MW00441899

# Easy-Sew Quilts
## *for* Urban Living

by Joanie Holton & Melanie Greseth for TailorMade by Design

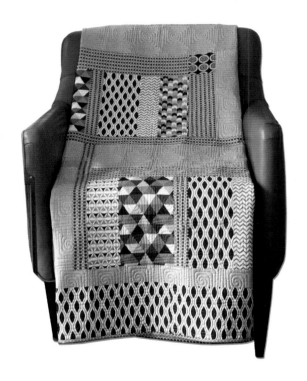

Landauer Publishing, LLC

# Easy-Sew Quilts
## *for* Urban Living

Copyright © 2015 by Landauer Publishing, LLC

Projects Copyright © 2015
by Joanie Holton and Melanie Greseth
for TailorMade by Design

This book was designed, produced,
and published by Landauer Publishing, LLC
3100 101st Street, Urbandale, IA 50322
www.landauerpub.com
515/287/2144   800/557/2144


President/Publisher: Jeramy Lanigan Landauer

Editor: Jeri Simon

Art Director: Laurel Albright

Photographer: Sue Voegtlin

Library of Congress Control Number: 2015938252

ISBN 13: 978-1-935726-74-6

This book printed on acid-free paper.

Printed in United States

10-9-8-7-6-5-4-3-2-1

 FACEBOOK.COM/
LANDAUERPUBLISHING
 YOUTUBE.COM/
LANDAUERPUBLISHING
 PINTEREST.COM/
LANDAUERPUB

# Introduction

The past few years we have enjoyed a new season of our lives as we have started to send our kids, nieces and nephews (aka: young adults) out into the world on their own. We designed the quilts in this book with our 20-somethings in mind. Their energy, playfulness and creativity inspire us and keep us young at heart. Each of these quilts took less than a day to put together and have a simple, contemporary styling for a relaxed, urban lifestyle. They are a perfect birthday, graduation, housewarming or wedding gift for a generation that still craves a bit of "home comfort" to wrap themselves in. We hope you find within these pages, a quilt for each of the 20-somethings in your life.

*Joanie & Melanie*

# Table of Contents

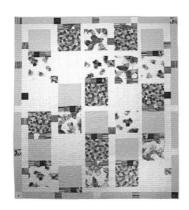

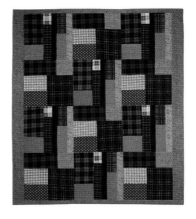

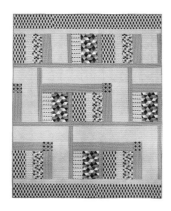

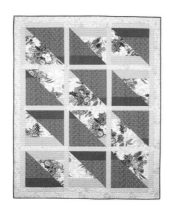
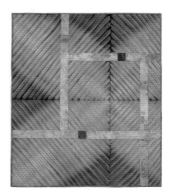

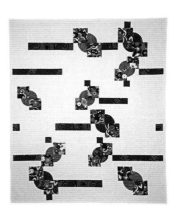
5

# Art in the Park Quilt

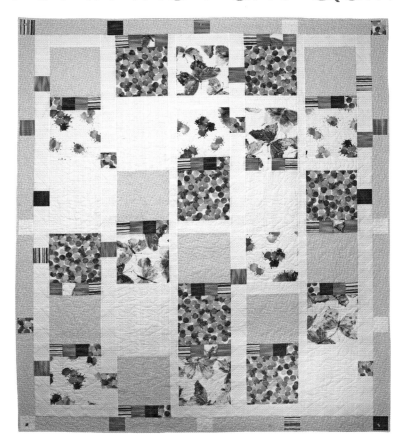

Designed and pieced by TailorMade by Design;
quilted by Naomi Polzin

Finished quilt size: 65" x 76-1/2"

## Yardage

5/8 yard paint splatter multi-color print fabric

7/8 yard circle multi-color print fabric

3/4 yard large butterfly multi-color print fabric

1/3 yard multi-color stripe fabric

1-3/4 yards white on white print fabric

1-2/3 yards yellow print fabric

3/8 yard green tonal print fabric

1/4 yard blue tonal print fabric

1/4 yard orange tonal print fabric

4 yards backing fabric

WOF = width of fabric

Read all instructions before beginning. Yardage is based on 44/45"-wide fabric. Cutting instructions include 1/4" seam allowance.

## Cutting

**Note:** As you cut, label each group of fabrics with its corresponding letter. This will help as you assemble the strip sets and block and sashing rows.

**From paint splatter multi-color print fabric, cut:**
(5) 9-1/2" A squares

**From circle multi-color print fabric, cut:**
(7) 9-1/2" A squares
(6) 3-1/4" F squares
(1) 2-3/4" x WOF D strip

**From large butterfly multi-color print fabric, cut:**
(5) 9-1/2" A squares
(1) 2-3/4" x WOF D strip

**From multi-color stripe fabric, cut:**
(2) 2-3/4" x WOF D strips
(4) 3-1/4" F squares

**From white on white print fabric, cut:**
(3) 9-1/2" x WOF strips. From the strips, cut:
    (4) 9-1/2" x 14" B rectangles
    (1) 9-1/2" x 11-3/4" C rectangle
    (11) 9-1/2" x 2-3/4" E strips

(7) 3-1/4" x WOF strips. Subcut the strips in the order given.
    From strip 1, cut: (1) 3-1/4" x 29-1/4" P strip
    From strip 2, cut: (2) 3-1/4" x 6-3/4" N strips and
        (1) 3-1/4" x 25" O strip
    From strip 3, cut: (1) 3-1/4" x 13-3/4" K strip and
        (1) 3 1/4" x 25" O strip
    From strip 4, cut: (1) 3-1/4" x 22" J strip and
        (1) 3-1/4" x 18-1/2" H strip
    From strip 5, cut: (1) 3-1/4" x 22" J strip and
        (1) 3-1/4" x 18-1/2" H strip
    From strip 6, cut: (5) 3-1/4" x 8" G strips
    From strip 7, cut: (1) 3-1/4" x 8" G strip,
        (1) 3-1/4" x 8-1/4" I strip, (1) 3-1/4" x 5-3/4" L
        strip and (6) 3-1/4" F squares

(4) 2" x WOF M strips.
    Sew (2) M strips together along a short edge to make one sashing strip. Repeat with the remaining pair of M strips. These strips are sashing columns 5 and 9.
**Note:** Due to variation of seam widths, these will not be trimmed until the pieced rows have been sewn together and measured during the quilt assembly process.

**From yellow print fabric, cut:**
(8) 9-1/2" A squares
(7) 3-1/4" x WOF strips. From the strips, cut:
    (8) 3-1/4" x 16" Q strips
    (4) 3-1/4" x 13-1/2" S strips
    (4) 3-1/4" x 13" R strips

(7) 2-1/4" x WOF binding strips

**From green tonal print fabric, cut:**
(2) 2-3/4" x WOF D strips
(7) 3-1/4" F squares

**From blue tonal print fabric, cut:**
(1) 2-3/4" x WOF D strip
(4) 3-1/4" F squares

**From orange tonal print fabric, cut:**
(1) 2-3/4" x WOF D strip
(3) 3-1/4" F squares

**From backing fabric, cut:**
(2) 72" x WOF pieces

# Sewing Instructions

**Note:** Press all seams in the same direction as you assemble strip sets, block and sashing columns and borders.

1. Referring to the diagram, lay out a circle multi-color print, blue tonal print, green tonal print and multi-color stripe 2-3/4" x WOF D strip in the order shown. Sew the strips together to make a strip set.

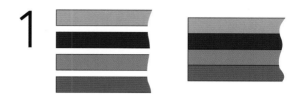

2. Subcut the strip set into (9) 2-3/4"- wide D1 segments.

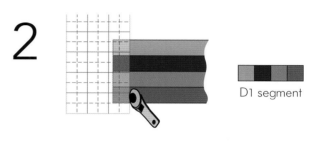

D1 segment

3. Referring to the diagram, lay out an orange tonal print, large butterfly multi-color print, green tonal print and multi-color stripe 2-3/4" x WOF D strip in the order shown. Sew the strips together to make a strip set.

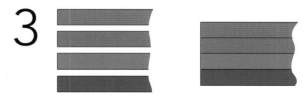

4. Subcut the strip set into (6) 2-3/4"-wide D2 segments.

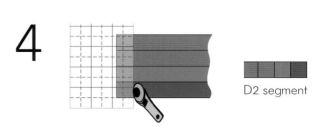

D2 segment

# Row Assembly

Lay out the pieces vertically in the order listed within each column and then sew the pieces together. Press all seams in one direction.

## sashing row 1 -

G white on white print strip

F green tonal print square

H white on white print strip

F blue tonal print square

I white on white print strip

F multi-stripe square

H white on white print strip

F green tonal print square

G white on white print strip

## block row 2 -

E white on white print rectangle

A yellow print square

D1 segment

A paint splatter multi-color print square

B white on white print rectangle

A circle multi-color print square

D2 segment

A yellow print square

D1 segment

A paint splatter multi-color print square

E white on white print rectangle

## sashing row 3 -

J white on white print strip

F circle multi-color print square

K white on white print strip

F green tonal print

J white on white print strip

F circle multi-color print square

L white on white print strip

## block row 4 -

D2 segment

A circle multi-color print square

B white on white print rectangle

A yellow print square

D1 segment

A large butterfly multi-color print square

B white on white print rectangle

A yellow print square

D1 segment

## sashing row 5 -

M white on white strip

**Note:** Measure rows 4 and 6 and trim row 5 to this measurement. You can also sew rows 4 and 6 to either side of row 5 and then trim.

M

## block row 6 -

E white on white print rectangle

A large butterfly multi-color print square

E white on white print rectangle

A paint splatter multi-color print square

D1 segment

A circle multi-color print square

E white on white print rectangle

A yellow print square

D1 segment

A circle multi-color print square

D2 segment

A large butterfly multi-color print square

E white on white print rectangle

## sashing row 7 -

N white on white print strip

F green tonal print square

N white on white print strip

F circle multi-color print square

O white on white print strip

F green tonal print square

O white on white print strip

## block row 8 -

D2 segment

A circle multi-color print square

E white on white print E rectangle

A large butterfly multi-color print square

D2 segment

C white on white rectangle

A paint splatter multi-color print square

E white on white print rectangle

A yellow print square

D1 segment

A circle multi-color print square

E white on white print rectangle

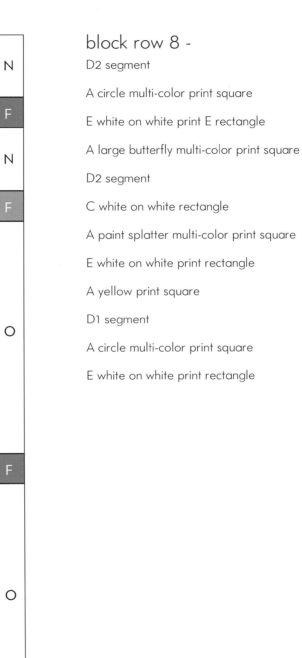

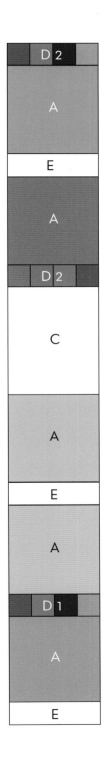

## sashing row 9 -

M white on white strip

**Note:** Measure rows 8 and 10 and trim row 9 to this measurement. You can also sew rows 8 and 10 to either side of row 9 and then trim.

M

## block row 10 -

E white on white print rectangle

A yellow print square

D1 segment

A paint splatter multi-color print square

E white on white print rectangle

A circle multi-color print square

D2 segment

A yellow print square

D1 segment

A large butterfly multi-color print square

B white on white print rectangle

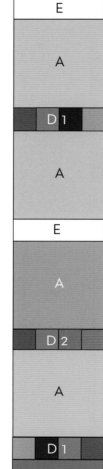

## sashing row 11 -

G white on white print strip

F multi-color stripe square

G white on white print strip

F green tonal print square

G white on white print strip

F blue tonal print square

P white on white print strip

F circle multi-color print square

G white on white print strip

G

F

G

F

G

F

P

F

G

# Quilt Center Assembly

Referring to the Quilt Assembly Diagram, sew the sashing and block rows together in pairs. Sew the pairs together and add sashing row 11 to complete the quilt center. Press the seams in one direction.

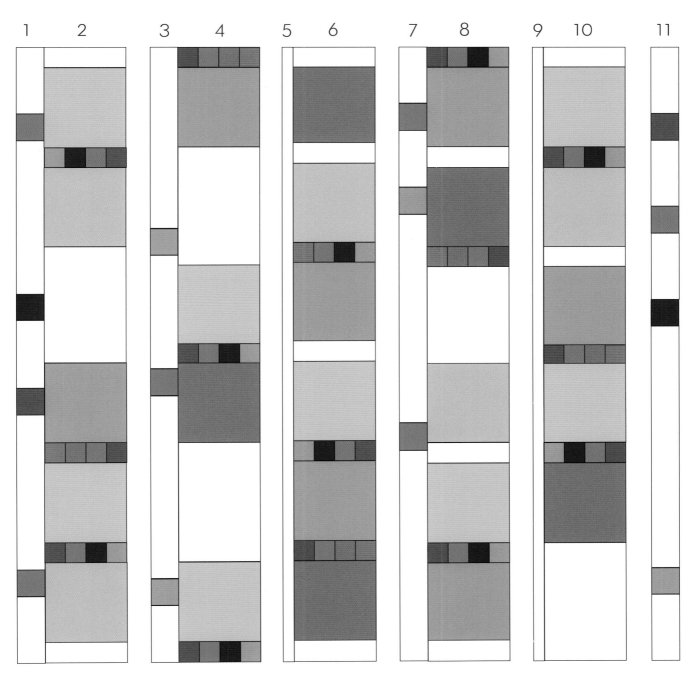

Quilt Assembly Diagram

## Border Assembly

Sew the pieces of each border together in the order given. Press the seams in one direction.

## left border -

Q yellow print strip

F orange tonal print square

Q yellow print strip

F white on white print square

Q yellow print strip

F circle multi-color print square

Q yellow print strip

## right border -

Q yellow print strip

F orange tonal print square

Q yellow print strip

F white on white print square

Q yellow print strip

F white on white print square

Q yellow print strip

## top border -

F multi-color stripe square

S yellow print strip

F blue tonal print square

R yellow print strip

F green tonal print square

R yellow print strip

F white on white print square

S yellow print strip

F circle multi-color print square

## bottom border -

F white on white print square

S yellow print strip

F orange tonal print square

R yellow print strip

F white on white print square

R yellow print strip

F multi-color stripe square

S yellow print strip

F blue tonal print square

Left    Right

Top    Bottom

# Quilt Top Assembly

1. Sew the left and right borders to opposite sides of the quilt center. Press the seams toward the borders. Trim borders even with quilt center if needed.

2. Sew the top and bottom borders to the top and bottom of the quilt center. Press the seams toward the borders. Trim borders even with quilt center if needed to complete the quilt top.

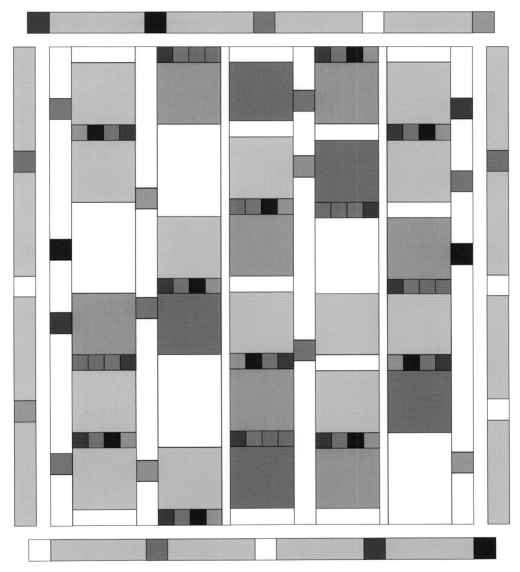

# Finishing

1. Sew the (2) 72" x WOF backing pieces together lengthwise. Press the seam open. Layer quilt top, batting and backing together and baste. Tie, hand or machine quilt as desired.

2. Sew the (7) 2-1/4" x WOF binding strips together into one continuous strip. Press the strip in half lengthwise, wrong sides together, and sew to the raw edge of the quilt top. Fold over raw edges and hand stitch in place on back of quilt.

# October Nights Quilt

Designed and pieced by TailorMade by Design;
quilted by Naomi Polzin

Finished quilt size: 62" x 75"

Finished block size: 18"

## Yardage

2/3 yard blue plaid flannel

1/2 yard red stripe flannel

1/4 yard taupe plaid flannel

1/2 yard black/red/tan plaid flannel

1/3 yard dark speckled flannel

1/3 yard red/multi-colored plaid flannel

3/8 yard green stripe flannel

3/8 yard mustard speckled flannel

5/8 yard red plaid flannel

3/8 yard taupe speckled flannel

3/8 yard red with white dots flannel

3/8 yard cream/multi-colored plaid flannel

7/8 yard green/red plaid flannel

1-1/3 yards green speckled flannel

3-3/4 yards backing fabric

WOF = width of fabric

Read all instructions before beginning. Yardage is based on 44/45"-wide fabric. Cutting instructions include 1/4" seam allowance.

**Note:** If using directional/novelty prints add 1/4 to 3/8 yard to yardage requirements.

Photo courtesy of Trina Severson, 507 Studio

## Cutting

**Note:** As you cut, label each group of fabrics with its corresponding letter. This will help as you assemble the blocks.

From blue plaid flannel, cut:
(6) 7-3/4" x 12-1/2" A rectangles

From red stripe flannel, cut:
(6) 7-3/4" x 6-1/2" B rectangles

From taupe plaid flannel, cut:
(6) 3-1/2" x 4-3/4" C rectangles

From black/tan/red plaid flannel, cut:
(6) 3-1/2" x 14-1/4" D strips

From dark speckled flannel, cut:
(6) 2-1/4" x 18-1/2" E strips

From red/multi-colored plaid flannel, cut:
(6) 4" x 8-1/4" F rectangles

From green stripe flannel, cut:
(6) 4" x 10-3/4" G strips

From mustard speckled flannel, cut:
(6) 3" x 18-1/2" H strips

From red plaid flannel, cut:
(6) 12-1/2" x 6-1/2" I rectangles

From taupe speckled flannel, cut:
(6) 6-1/2" J squares

From red with white dots flannel, cut:
(6) 9" x 6-1/2" K rectangles

From cream/multi-colored plaid flannel, cut:
(6) 9" x 6-1/2" L rectangles

From green/red plaid flannel, cut:
(6) 10" x 12-1/2" M rectangles

From green speckled flannel, cut:
(4) 4-1/2" x WOF side border strips
(3) 2" x WOF top and bottom border strips
(7) 2-1/4" x WOF binding strips

From backing fabric, cut:
(2) 67-1/2" x WOF pieces

# Block Assembly

Lay out the pieces in the order listed within each column and then sew the pieces together. Press all seams in one direction.

## Block 1 Segments

A blue plaid rectangle

B red stripe rectangle

C taupe plaid rectangle

D black/tan/red plaid strip

E dark speckled strip

F red/multi-colored plaid rectangle

G green stripe rectangle

H mustard speckled strip

Sew the segments together to make Block 1. Make a total of 6 Block 1.

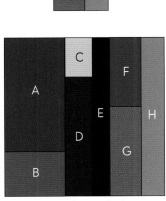

Make 6 Block 1

## Block 2 Segments

I red plaid rectangle

J taupe speckled square

L cream/multi-colored plaid rectangle

K red with white dots rectangle

M green/red plaid rectangle

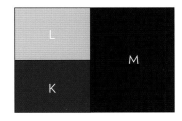

Sew the segments together to make Block 2. Make a total of 6 Block 2.

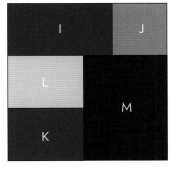

Make 6 Block 2

# Quilt Center Assembly

1. Referring to the Row Assembly Diagram, lay out the blocks in 4 rows with 3 blocks in each row. Alternate the blocks in each row. Rows 1 and 3 begin with Block 1 and rows 2 and 4 begin with Block 2.

2. Sew the blocks together in rows. Press the seams in rows 1 and 3 to the right and the seams in rows 2 and 4 to the left.

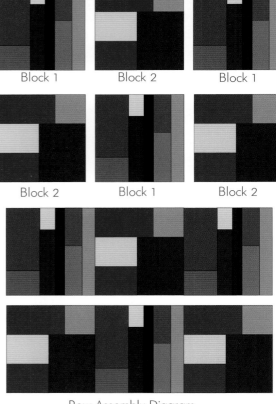

Block 1          Block 2          Block 1

Block 2          Block 1          Block 2

Row Assembly Diagram

3. Sew rows together to complete the quilt center.

Quilt Center Assembly Diagram

## Border and Quilt Assembly

1. Sew (2) 4-1/2" x WOF green speckled strips together along the short ends. Press the seam open to complete a side border. Make 2 side borders.

2. Sew the side borders to opposite sides of the quilt center. Trim the side borders even with wthe quilt top and bottom. Press the seams toward the borders.

3. Sew (2) 2" x WOF green speckled strips together along the short ends. Press the seam open.

4. Sew the strip to the top of the quilt center. Trim even with the quilt sides and press seams toward the border.

5. Sew the trimmed strip to the remaining 2" x WOF green speckled strip. Press the seam open. Sew the strip to the bottom of the quilt center. Trim even with quilt sides and press seams toward the border to complete the quilt top.

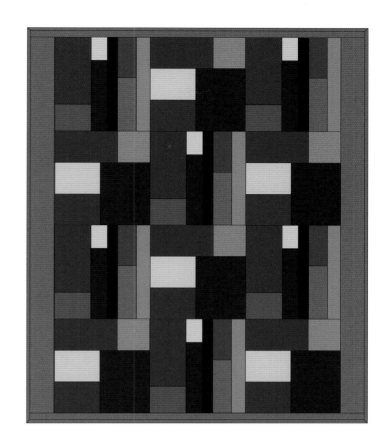

## Finishing

1. Sew the (2) 67-1/2" x WOF backing pieces together lengthwise. Press seam open. Layer quilt top, batting and backing together and baste. Tie, hand or machine quilt as desired.

2. Sew the (7) 2-1/4" x WOF binding strips together into one continuous strip. Press the binding strip in half lengthwise, wrong sides together, and sew to the raw edge of the quilt top. Fold over raw edges and hand stitch in place on back of quilt.

Photo courtesy of Trina Severson, 507 Studio

# City Blocks Quilt

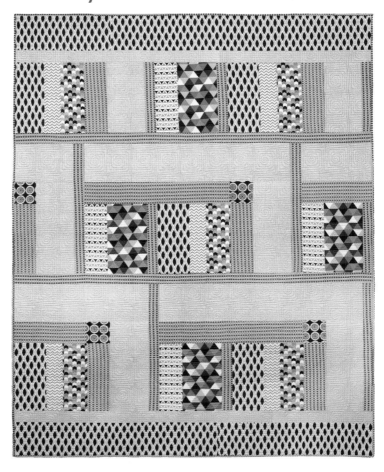

Designed and pieced by TailorMade by Design;
quilted by Sheri Zalar

Finished quilt size: 60-1/2" x 77"

## Yardage

Fat 1/8 navy sunburst print fabric

5/8 yard blue tonal hexagon print fabric

3/8 yard blue/green/white arrow print fabric

1/3 yard gray/blue zigzag print fabric

1-1/8 yards navy curve print fabric

5/8 yard large blue tonal triangle print fabric

3/8 yard blue/gray/green geometric print fabric

1-5/8 yards gray metallic fabric

1-1/8 yards gray tonal hexagon print fabric

3-3/4 yards backing fabric

WOF = width of fabric
Fat eighth = 9" x 22"
Read all instructions before beginning. Yardage is based on 44/45"-wide fabric. Cutting instructions include 1/4" seam allowance.

Photo courtesy of Trina Severson, 507 Studio

## Cutting

**Note:** As you cut, label each group of fabrics with its corresponding letter. This will help as you assemble the blocks and sets.

**From navy sunburst print fabric, cut:**
(4) 4-1/4" B squares

**From blue tonal hexagon print fabric, cut:**
(2) 4-1/4" x 24-1/2" C2 strips
(7) 4-1/4" x 12-1/2" C1 strips
(1) 4-1/4" x 12-1/4" C3 strip

**From blue/green/white arrow print fabric, cut:**
(5) 4-1/4" x 12-1/2" P strips

**From gray/blue zigzag print fabric, cut:**
(5) 3-1/4" x 12-1/2" Q strips

**From navy curve print fabric, cut:**
(5) 5-3/4" x 12-1/2" R strips
(3) 6-1/2" x WOF I border strips

**From large blue tonal triangle print fabric, cut:**
(4) 7" x 12-1/2" S strips

**From blue/gray/green geometric print fabric, cut:**
(4) 4-1/4" x 12-1/2" T strips

**From gray metallic fabric, cut:**
(4) 6-3/4" x 16-1/4" A rectangles
(2) 6-3/4" x 12-1/2" L rectangles
(2) 7" x 34-1/2" D1 strips
(1) 7" x 22-1/2" D2 strip
(1) 7" x 12-1/2" D3 strip
(1) 7" x 10-1/2" D4 strip
(3) 2-1/2" x WOF H border strips

**From gray tonal hexagon print fabric, cut:**
(15) 2-1/4" x WOF strips. From 2 strips, cut:
    (6) 2-1/4" x 12-1/2" K strips
    From remaining strips, cut:
    (4) 2-1/4" x 22-3/4" F strips
    (2) 2-1/4" x WOF G strips. Sew the remaining portions of 2 F strips to the ends of 2 G strips to make 2 continuous strips.
(7) 2-1/4" x WOF binding strips

**From backing fabric cut:**
(2) 66" x WOF pieces

# Block Assembly

Lay out the pieces in the order listed within each column and then sew the pieces together. Press all seams in one direction.

**Note:** Label the blocks as they are completed.

## Block A

B navy sunburst square

C1 blue tonal hexagon strip

A gray metallic rectangle

Sew the segments together to make Block A. Make a total of 4 Block A.

Block A

## Block B

R navy curve strip

Q gray/blue zigzag strip

P blue/green/white arrow strip

Sew the segments together to make Block B. Make a total of 5 Block B.

Block B

## Block C

T blue/gray/green geometric

S blue tonal triangle strip

K gray tonal hexagon strip

Sew the segments together to make Block C. Make a total of 4 Block C.

Block C

## Block D

C1 blue tonal hexagon strip

L gray metallic rectangle

K gray tonal hexagon strip

Sew the segments together to make Block D. Make a total of 2 Block D.

Block D

# Set Assembly

Lay out the pieces in the order listed within each column and then sew the pieces together. Press all seams in one direction.

## Set 1

Block C to Block B

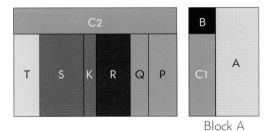

Block C    Block B

C2 blue tonal hexagon strip to the top of block unit

A Block to the block unit

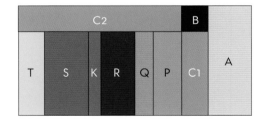

Block A

D1 gray metallic strip to the top of the block units

F gray tonal hexagon strip to the unit to make Set 1.
Make a total of 2 Set 1.

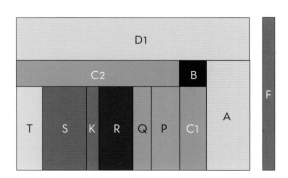

# Set 2

C3 blue tonal hexagon strip to Block B

Block unit to Block A

Block A

D2 gray metallic strip to block unit

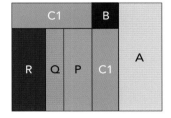

F gray tonal hexagon strip to the unit to make Set 2

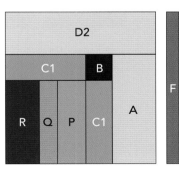

Set 2

## Set 3

C1 blue tonal hexagon strip to
Block C

D3 gray metallic strip to block
unit to make Set 3

## Set 4

D4 gray metallic strip to Block A

F gray metallic strip to block unit
to make Set 4.

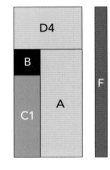

## Quilt Center Rows

Lay out the blocks and sets in three rows as shown.

Row 1 – Block B, Block D,
Block C, Block B and Block D

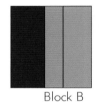
Block B

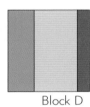
Block D

Block C

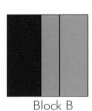
Block B

Block D

Row 2 – Set 4, Set 1 and Set 3

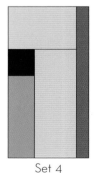
Set 4

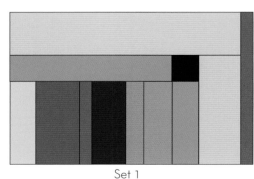
Set 1

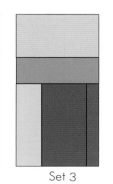
Set 3

Row 3 – Set 2 and Set 1

Sew the blocks and sets together in rows.

Set 2                    Set 1

## Quilt Center Assembly and Borders

1. Measure the width of each row; the measurements should be the same. Cut the gray tonal hexagon G strips to your row measurement.

2. Sew the strips to the top of rows 2 and 3.

3. Sew the rows together to complete the quilt center.

4. Sew the 3 navy curve 6-1/2" x WOF I strips together along the short ends to make one continuous strip. Repeat for the 3 gray metallic 2-1/2" x WOF H strips.

5. Using the row measurement in Step 1, cut the strips in Step 4 to this measurement.

6. Sew an H and I strip together along one long edge to make a border strip. Make 2 border strips.

7. Sew the border strips to the top and bottom of the quilt center. The navy curve I strips should be on the outer edges.

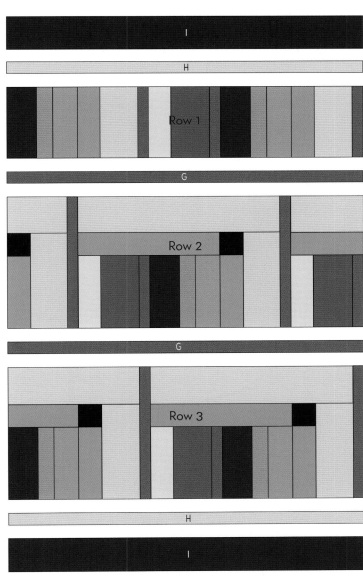

## Finishing

1. Sew the (2) 66" x WOF backing pieces together lengthwise. Press seam open. Layer quilt top, batting and backing together and baste. Tie, hand or machine quilt as desired.

2. Sew the (7) 2-1/4" x WOF binding strips together into one continuous strip. Press the strip in half lengthwise, wrong sides together, and sew to the raw edge of the quilt top. Fold over raw edges and hand stitch in place on back of quilt.

# Urban Retro Quilt

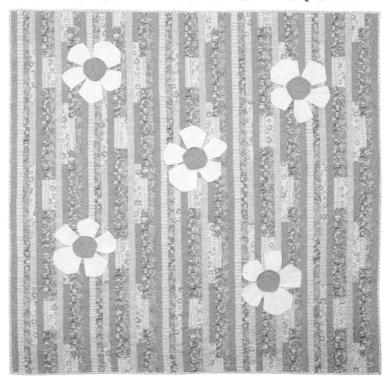

Designed and pieced by TailorMade by Design;
quilted by Sue Krause

Finished quilt size: 57" x 60-1/2"

Finished block size: 8" x 10"

## Yardage

1-1/8 yards pink vine stripe fabric

1-1/8 yards spring floral (white flower on green/pink) fabric

1-1/2 yards green tonal fabric

7/8 yard pink wavy stripe fabric

1 yard pink tonal flower fabric

1-3/4 yards dark pink tonal dot fabric

3/4 yard white tonal fabric

3-1/2 yards backing fabric

WOF = width of fabric
Read all instructions before beginning. Yardage is based on 44/45"-wide fabric. Cutting instructions include 1/4" seam allowance.

## Cutting

**Note:** As you cut, label each group of fabrics with its measurements. This will help as you assemble the blocks and sets.

**From pink vine stripe fabric, cut:**
(3) 3" x WOF strips
(8) 1-1/2" x WOF sashing strips
(6) 2-1/4" x WOF binding strips

**From spring floral fabric, cut:**
(3) 8" x WOF strips
(2) 3" x WOF strips

**From green tonal fabric, cut:**
(4) 8" x WOF strips
(8) 1-1/2" x WOF sashing strips

**From pink wavy stripe fabric, cut:**
(30) 1-1/2" x 10-1/2" #6 strips
(2) 5-1/2" x WOF strips

**From pink tonal floral fabric, cut:**
(4) 5-1/2" x WOF strips
(2) 3" x WOF strips

**From dark pink tonal dot fabric, cut:**
(30) 1-1/2" x 10-1/2" #3 strips
(2) 5-1/2" x WOF strips
(9) 1-1/2" x WOF sashing strips
(10) center circles using the template on page 41

**From white tonal fabric, cut:**
(10) each 1, 2, 3, 4, 5 petals using the templates on pages 40-41

**From backing fabric, cut:**
(2) 63" x WOF pieces

Photo courtesy of
Trina Severson, 507 Studio

# Segment Assembly

**Note:** Label the segments as you cut them. Segments #3 and #6 are solid strips and have already been cut.

1. Sew an 8" x WOF green tonal strip and a 3" x WOF spring floral strip together along one long edge to make a strip set. Make a total of 2 strip sets. Cut the strip sets into (30) 1-1/2" x 10-1/2" segments. Label the segments #1.

2. Sew a 5-1/2" x WOF pink wavy strip and a 5-1/2" x WOF pink tonal floral strip together along one long edge to make a strip set. Make a total of 2 strip sets. Cut the strip sets into (30) 1-1/2" x 10-1/2" segments. Label the segments #2.

3. Sew an 8" x WOF spring floral strip and a 3" x WOF pink vine strip together along one long edge to make a strip set. Make a total of 3 strip sets. Cut the strip sets into (60) 1-1/2" x 10-1/2" segments. Label 30 segments #4 and 30 segments #8.

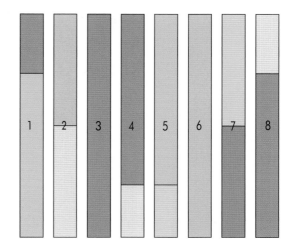

4. Sew an 8" x WOF green tonal strip and a 3" x WOF pink tonal floral strip together along one long edge to make a strip set. Make a total of 2 strip sets. Cut the strip sets into (30) 1-1/2" x 10-1/2" segments. Label the segments #5.

5. Sew a 5-1/2" x WOF pink tonal floral strip and a 5-1/2" x WOF dark pink tonal dot strip together along one long edge to make a strip set. Make a total of 2 sets. Cut the strip sets into (30) 1-1/2" x 10-1/2" segments. Label the segments #7.

# Block Assembly

1. Referring to the Block A Diagram, lay out the segments as shown. Pay attention to the position of each segment.

2. Sew the segments together to make Block A. Make a total of 15 Block A. Press all seams to the right.

3. Referring to the Block B Diagram, lay out the segments as shown. Pay attention to the position of each segment.

4. Sew the segments together to make Block B. Make a total of 15 Block B. Press all seams to the left.

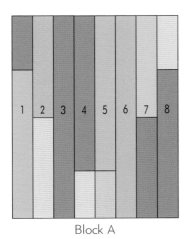

Block A

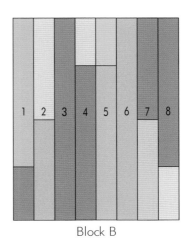

Block B

# Row Assembly

1. Referring to the Row Assembly Diagram, lay out the A and B Blocks in 5 vertical rows with 6 blocks in each row. The blocks alternate within each row.

2. Sew the blocks together in vertical rows.

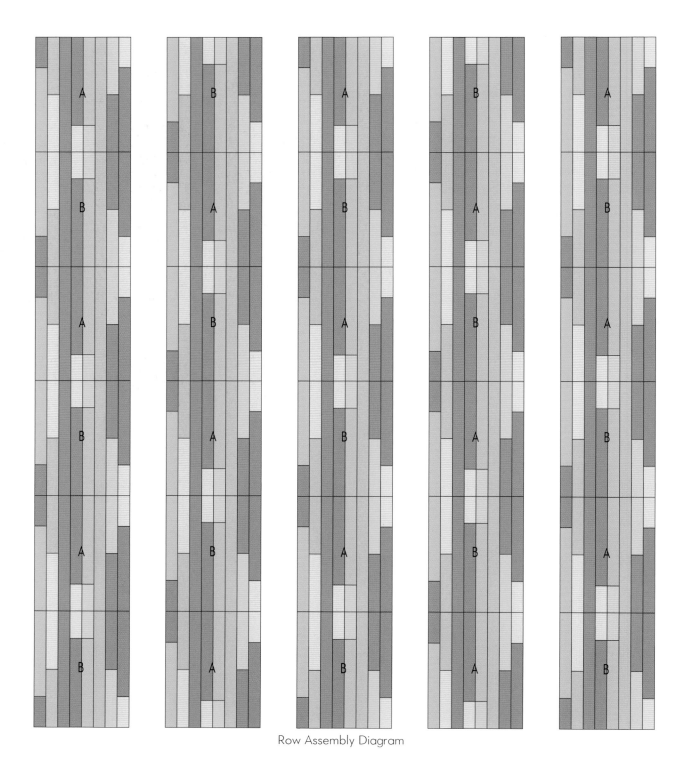

Row Assembly Diagram

# Sashing Set Assembly

1.  Sew the green tonal 1-1/2" x WOF sashing strips together along the short ends to make one continuous sashing strip.

2.  Referring to step 1, sew the pink vine stripe and dark pink tonal dot 1-1/2" x WOF sashing strips together in the same manner.

3.  Measure the block rows and cut 5 green tonal, 6 dark pink tonal dot and 5 pink vine stripe sashing strips to this measurement.

4.  Sew a green tonal, dark pink tonal dot and pink vine stripe sashing strip together as shown to make a center sashing set. Make a total of 4 **center** sashing sets.

5.  Sew a dark pink tonal dot and pink vine stripe sashing strip together to make a **left** sashing set.

6.  Sew a green tonal and dark pink tonal dot sashing strip together to make a **right** sashing set.

Photo courtesy of Trina Severson, 507 Studio

Center
Sashing
Set

Left
Sashing
Set

Right
Sashing
Set

# Quilt Assembly

1.  Referring to the Quilt Assembly Diagram, lay out the rows and center sashing sets as shown.

2.  Sew the pieces together to complete the quilt center.

3.  Sew the left sashing set to the left edge of the quilt center. Sew the right sashing set to the right side of the quilt center to complete the quilt top.

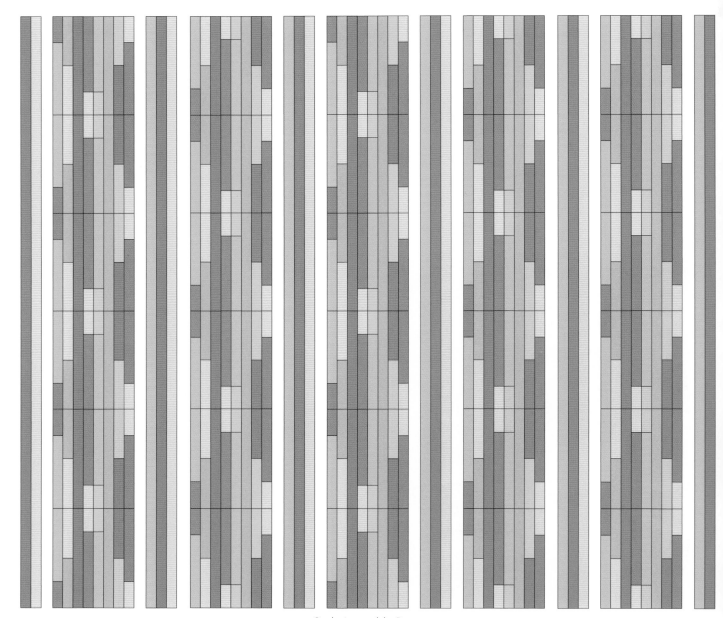

Quilt Assembly Diagram

# Finishing

1. Sew the (2) 63" x WOF backing pieces together lengthwise. Press the seam open. Layer quilt top, batting and backing together and baste. Tie, hand or machine quilt as desired.

2. Sew the (6) 2-1/4" x WOF binding strips together into one continuous strip. Press the strip in half lengthwise, wrong sides together, and sew to the raw edge of the quilt top. Fold over raw edges and hand stitch in place on back of quilt.

# Flower Assembly

**Note:** The flowers are added after the quilting has been completed.

1. Sew 2 petal 1 pieces right sides together. Leave the bottom of the petal open. Turn the petal right side out and press.

2. Repeat step 1 for the remaining petal and center circle pieces. Slipstitch the center circle openings closed. Number the petals as they are completed.

3. Referring to the diagram for placement, arrange the flowers on the quilt using petals 1-5 in each flower. Place a center circle over the middle of the petals. Pin the flower pieces in place.

4. Stitch around the outer edge of the center circle catching the bottoms of each petal with the stitching. Secure the petals with stitching loops and lines as shown in the photograph on page 32.

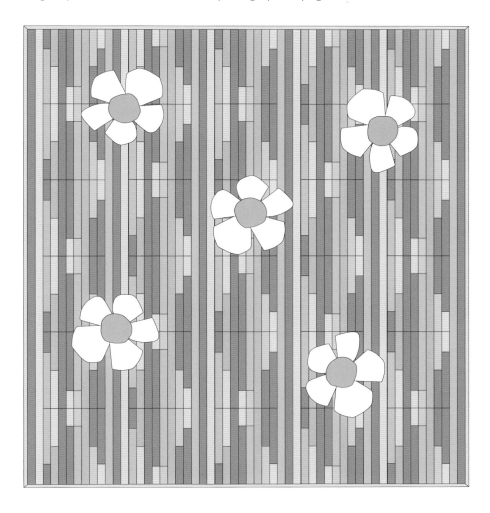

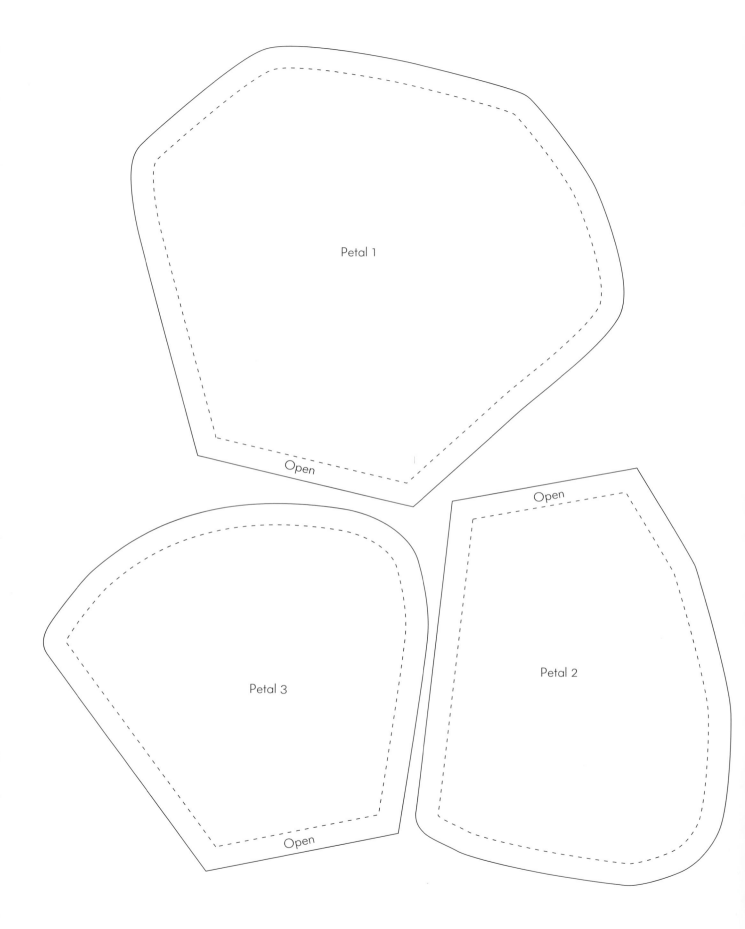

Petal 1

Open

Petal 3

Open

Open

Petal 2

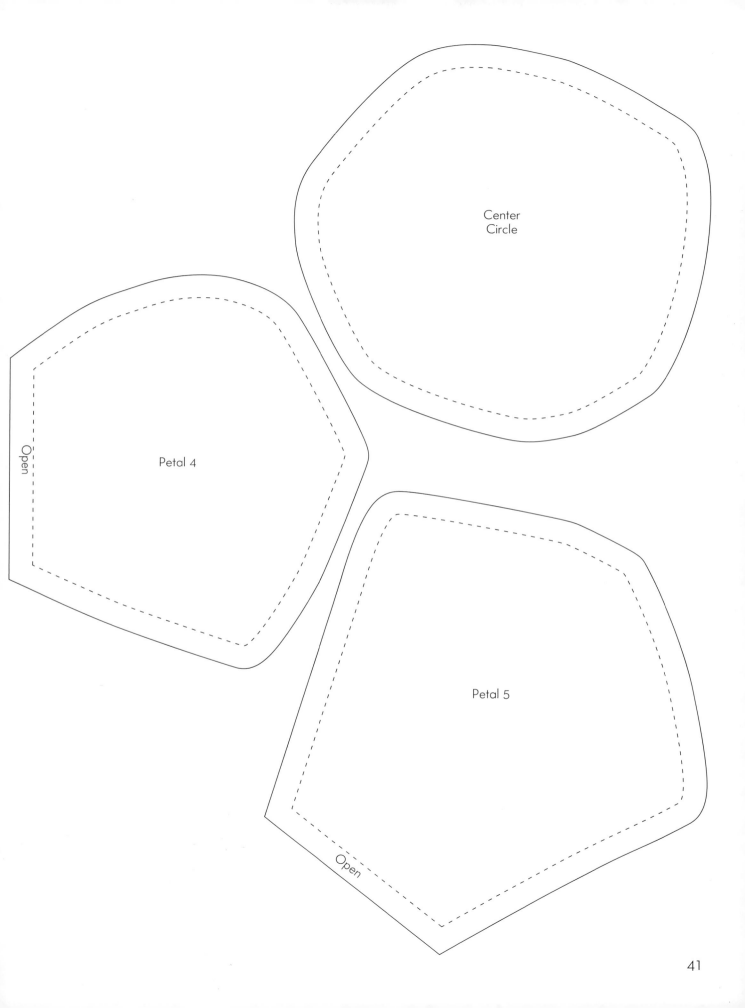

Center
Circle

Open

Petal 4

Petal 5

Open

# Community Garden Quilt

Designed and pieced by TailorMade by Design;
quilted by Sue Krause

Finished quilt size: 59" x 76"

Finished block size: 15" square

## Yardage

1-1/8 yards medium red print fabric

1 yard dark red print fabric

1-1/8 yards large floral print fabric

1/2 yard gray tonal print fabric

1 yard gold tonal print fabric

1 yard cream/gray print fabric

3-3/4 yards backing fabric

WOF = width of fabric
Read all instructions before beginning. Yardage is based on 44/45"-wide fabric. Cutting instructions include 1/4" seam allowance.

Photo courtesy of Trina Severson, 507 Studio

## Cutting

Lightly starch the fabrics before cutting.

**Note:** As you cut, label each group of fabrics with its corresponding letter. This will help as you assemble the sets.

**From medium red print fabric, cut:**
(6) 12-1/4" x 16" A rectangles

**From dark red print fabric, cut:**
(6) 4-1/4" x 16" B rectangles
(8) 2-1/4" x WOF binding strips

**From large floral print fabric, cut:**
(6) 12-1/4" x 16" A rectangles

**From gray tonal print fabric, cut:**
(6) 4-1/4" x 16" B rectangles

**From gold tonal print fabric, cut:**
(24) 2-1/2" x 15-1/2" C strips

**From cream/gray print fabric, cut:**
(7) 2-1/2" x 19-1/2" D strips
(6) 2-1/2" E square
(7) 3" x WOF border strips

**From backing fabric, cut:**
(2) 67-1/2" x WOF pieces

# Set Assembly

**Note:** As you sew, label each set with the corresponding its letter. This will help as you assemble the rows.

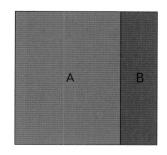

1. Sew a medium red A rectangle to a dark red B rectangle. Press the seam toward A to make an AB set. Square the AB set to 16". Make a total of 6 AB sets.

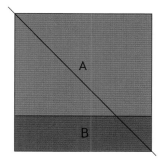
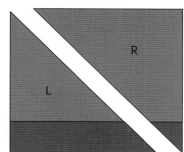

2. With the B rectangle at the bottom, cut the AB set diagonally from top left corner to bottom right corner. Label the left triangle section L and the right triangle section R. Make a total of 6 red L triangles and 6 red R triangles.

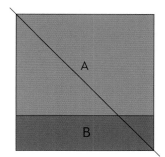
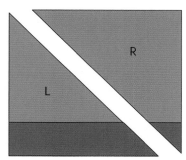

3. Referring to steps 1-2, use the gray floral A and gray tonal B rectangles to make a total of 6 gray L triangles and 6 gray R triangles.

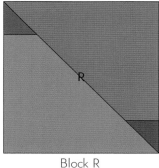

Block R

4. With right sides together, sew a gray R triangle to a red R triangle along the long edge as shown. Press the seam toward the red triangle to make a Block R. Make a total of 6 Block R. Square the blocks to 15-1/2".

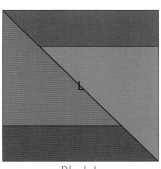

Block L

5. Referring to step 4, use a gray and red L triangle to make a total of 6 Block L. Square the blocks to 15-1/2".

## Sashing Assembly

1. Sew a cream/gray E square to one end of a gold tonal C strip. Press seam toward the C strip. Make a total of 6 EC sets.

| E | C |
|---|---|

2. Lay out a cream/gray D strip and 2 EC sets as shown. Sew the pieces together to make an ECD sashing strip. Press all seams toward the C strips. Make a total of 3 ECD sashing strips.

| E | C | D | C | E |
|---|---|---|---|---|

3. Sew a cream/gray D strip to opposite ends of a gold tonal C strip. Press to make a DCD sashing strip. Press all seams toward the C strip. Make a total of 2 DCD sashing strips.

| D | C | D |
|---|---|---|

## Row Assembly

1. Referring to the Quilt Center Assembly Diagram, lay out the blocks and gold tonal C strips in 4 rows as shown. Carefully watch the orientation of the blocks within each row.

2. Sew the pieces together in rows.

## Quilt Center Assembly

1. Lay out the block rows and sashing strips as shown in the Quilt Center Assembly Diagram.

2. Sew the pieces together to complete the quilt center.

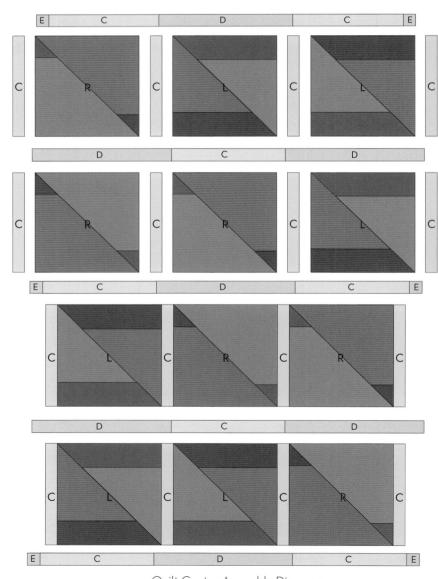

Quilt Center Assembly Diagram

## Border and Quilt Assembly

1.  Sew (2) 3" x WOF cream/gray strips together along the short ends. Press the seam open to complete a side border. Make 2 side borders.

2.  Sew the side borders to opposite sides of the quilt center. Trim the side borders even with the quilt top and bottom. Press the seams toward the borders.

3.  Sew (2) 3" x WOF cream/gray strips together along the short ends to make the top border. Press the seam open.

4.  Sew the strip to the top of the quilt center. Trim even with the quilt sides and press seams toward the border.

5.  Sew the trimmed strip to the remaining 3" x WOF cream/gray strip to make the bottom border. Press the seam open. Sew the bottom border to the bottom of the quilt center. Trim it even with quilt sides and press seams toward border to complete the quilt top.

## Finishing

1.  Sew the (2) 67-1/2" x WOF backing pieces together lengthwise. Press seam open. Layer quilt top, batting and backing together and baste. Tie, hand or machine quilt as desired.

2.  Sew the (8) 2-1/4" x WOF binding strips together into one continuous strip. Press the strip in half lengthwise, wrong sides together, and sew to the raw edge of the quilt top. Fold over raw edges and hand stitch in place on back of quilt.

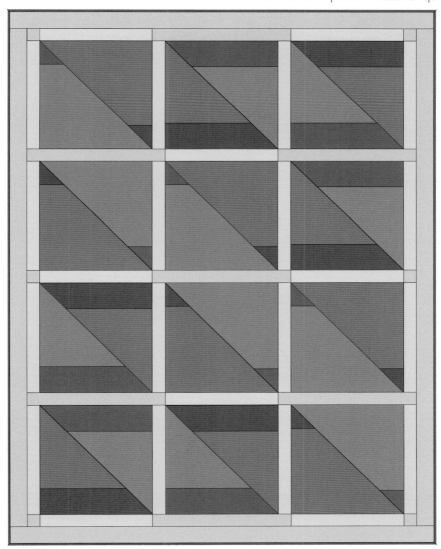

# Night in the City Wallhanging

Designed and pieced by TailorMade by Design;
quilted by Sue Krause

Finished wallhanging size: 36-1/2" x 43-1/2"

## Yardage

1-1/4 yards graphic print fabric

1/4 yard yellow/tan fabric

1/4 yard yellow/orange fabric

3" scrap green tonal fabric

3" scrap dark blue tonal fabric

3" scrap light blue tonal fabric

3/8 yard orange tonal fabric

1-1/2 yards backing fabric

Read all instructions before beginning. Yardage is based on 44/45"-wide fabric. Cutting instructions include 1/4" seam allowance.

## Cutting

From graphic print fabric—refer to the cutting diagram and use a chalk marker to draw cutting lines before cutting:
(1) 12-1/2" x 35-1/2" A rectangle.
  From the rectangle, subcut:
  (1) 3-1/2" x 12-1/2" B rectangle
**Note:** After subcutting, the remaining 12-1/2" x 32" section represents the A rectangle.
(1) 12-1/2" x 30" C rectangle
(1) 10-1/2" x 23" D rectangle
(1) 18" x 21-1/2 E rectangle.
  From the rectangle, subcut:
  (1) 3-1/2" x 18" F rectangle
**Note:** After subcutting, E represents the 18" center square.

From yellow/tan fabric, cut:
(1) 2-1/2" x 5-1/2" F1 strip
(1) 2-1/2" x 11" F2 strip
(2) 2-1/2" x 12-1/2" G1 strips
(1) 2-1/2" x 9" G2 strip

From yellow/orange fabric, cut:
(1) 2-1/2" x 6" H1 strip
(1) 2-1/2" x 22-1/2" H2 strip
(1) 2-1/2" x 17" J1 strip
(1) 2-1/2" x 18-1/2" J2 strip

From each 3" scrap fabric, cut:
(1) 2-1/2" square

From orange tonal fabric, cut:
(1) 2-1/2" square
(4) 2-1/4" x WOF binding strips

### Cutting Diagram
After drawing the cutting lines with chalk, cut the pieces in A-F sequence.

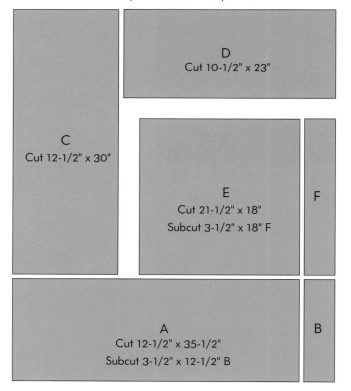

D
Cut 10-1/2" x 23"

C
Cut 12-1/2" x 30"

E
Cut 21-1/2" x 18"
Subcut 3-1/2" x 18" F

F

A
Cut 12-1/2" x 35-1/2"
Subcut 3-1/2" x 12-1/2" B

B

## Set Assembly

1. Sew yellow/tan F1 strip, orange 2-1/2"
   square and yellow/tan F2 strip together.
   Press seams toward strips to make an F set.

F set

2. Sew yellow/tan G1 strip, dark blue 2-1/2"
   square and yellow/tan G2 strip together.
   Press seams toward strips to make a G set.

G set

3. Sew yellow/orange H1 strip, green 2-1/2" square and
   yellow/orange H2 strip together. Press seams toward
   strips to make H set.

H set

4. Sew yellow/orange J1 strip, light blue 2-1/2" square and
   yellow/orange J2 strip together. Press seams toward
   strips to make a J set.

J set

## Quilt Top Assembly

Note: The quilt is assembled like a log cabin block. Refer to the diagrams for placement.

1. Sew the center square, F set and F rectangle
   together as shown to make a center unit.

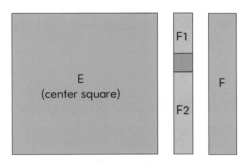

Center unit

2. Sew the D rectangle and G set together as shown to
   make a B unit.

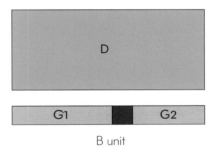

B unit

3. Sew the B unit to the top of the center unit.

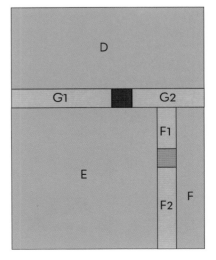

4.  Sew the C rectangle and H set together as shown to make a C unit. Sew the C unit to the left side of the unit made in step 3.

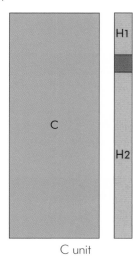

C unit

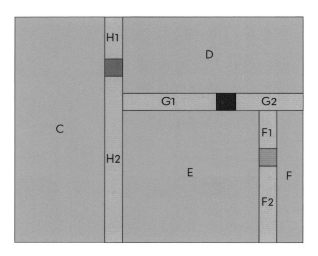

5.  Sew the A rectangle, G1 strip and B rectangle together as shown to make a D unit.

Photo courtesy of Trina Severson, 507 Studio

D unit

6.  Sew the J set to the top of the D unit.

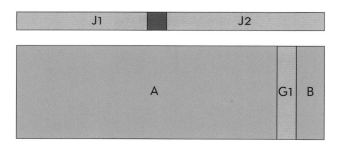

7.  To align the seam lines of the G1 and F2 strips, draw chalk lines on the wrong side of the J2 strip matching the seam lines of the G1 strip.

8. Sew the step 4 and 6 units together, matching the chalk lines, to finish the wallhanging top.

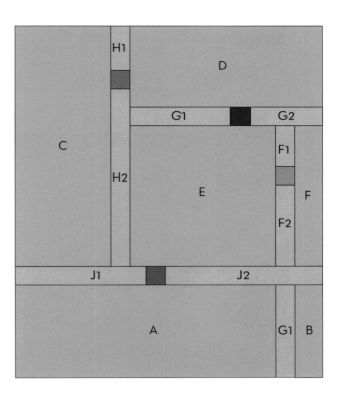

## Finishing

1. Layer wallhanging top, batting and backing together and baste. Tie, hand or machine quilt as desired.

2. Sew the (4) 2-1/4" x WOF binding strips together into one continuous strip. Press the strip in half lengthwise, wrong sides together, and sew to the raw edge of the quilt top. Fold over raw edges and hand stitch in place on back of quilt.

# New Direction Quilt

Designed and pieced by TailorMade by Design;
quilted by Sue Krause

Finished quilt size: 67-1/2" x 88"

## Yardage

1-3/4 yards charcoal dot fabric

1-1/4 yards white tonal fabric

1/4 yard green print fabric

3/4 yard gray tonal fabric

1-1/8 yards lilac tonal fabric

1/3 yard purple dot fabric

1-1/2 yards geometric print fabric

1/4 yard green dot fabric

1 yard gray/silver print fabric

3/4 yard gray/silver leaf fabric

1/4 yard black tonal fabric

4-1/2 yards backing fabric

WOF = width of fabric
Read all instructions before beginning. Yardage is based on 44/45"-wide fabric. Cutting instructions include 1/4" seam allowance.

Photo courtesy of Trina Severson, 507 Studio

## Cutting

**Note:** As you cut, label each group of fabrics with its corresponding number/letter. This will help as you assemble the quilt center.

**From charcoal dot fabric, cut:**
(1) 17" A square. Cut the square in half diagonally to make 2 A triangles.
(1) 15" x 36" 10A rectangle
(4) 2" x WOF border strips
(9) 2-1/4" x WOF binding strips

**From white tonal fabric, cut:**
(1) 4" x 23" 2A strip
(1) 4" x 26" 2B strip
(1) 4" x 36-1/2" 9A strip
(1) 9" x 13" 9B strip
(2) 4-1/2" x WOF border strips
(2) 3" x WOF border strips

**From green print fabric, cut:**
(2) 2-1/2" x 28" 3A, 3B strips

**From gray tonal fabric, cut:**
(1) 10" x 39" 4A rectangle
(1) 10" x 35" 4B rectangle

**From lilac tonal fabric, cut:**
(1) 12-1/2" x 48-1/2" 5A rectangle
(1) 12-1/2" x 37" 5B rectangle

**From purple dot fabric, cut:**
(1) 2-1/2" x 48-1/2" 6A strip
(1) 2-1/2" x 27" 6B strip

**From geometric print fabric, cut:**
(1) 16" x 48-1/2" 7A rectangle
(1) 16" x WOF 7B rectangle

**From green dot fabric, cut:**
(1) 2-1/2" x 37" 8A strip
(1) 2-1/2" x 13" 8B strip

**From gray/silver print fabric, cut:**
(2) 16" x WOF border strips

**From gray/silver leaf fabric, cut:**
(2) 11-1/2" x WOF border strips

**From black tonal fabric, cut:**
(2) 3-1/2" x WOF border strips

**From backing fabric, cut:**
(2) 74" x WOF pieces

# Quilt Center Assembly

**Note:** The strips and rectangles will not finish evenly. The ends will be trimmed beginning with step 7.

1. Placing an A triangle on its base with the point up. Label the right angle A and the left angle B. The A strips and rectangles will be sewn to the A side and the B strips and rectangles will be sewn to the B side.

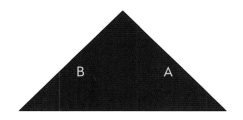

2. Aligning the top and side raw edges, sew a white tonal 2A strip to the A side of the charcoal dot A triangle. Press seams toward the strip.

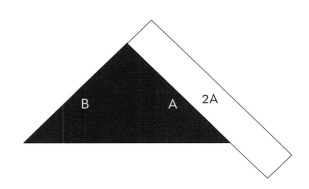

3. Aligning the top raw edge with the 2A strip, sew a white tonal 2B strip to the B side of the charcoal dot A triangle. Press seams toward the strip.

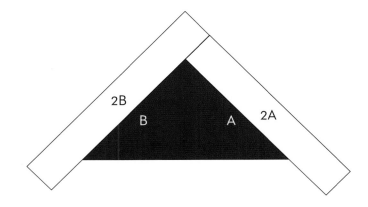

4. Referring to steps 2-3, sew the 3A/3B through 7A/7B strips and rectangles to the A triangle to make the quilt center.

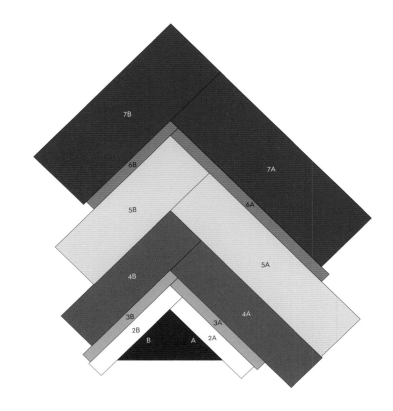

5. Lay the quilt center on a flat cutting surface with the A triangle base on the left. The B section will be at the top and the A section at the bottom.

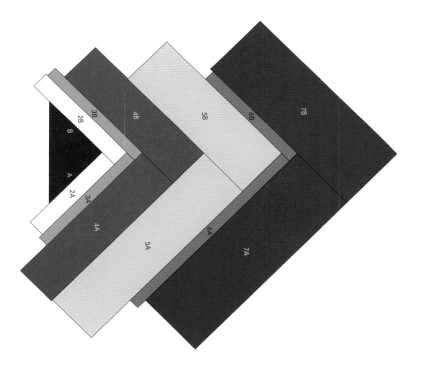

6. Referring to Trimming the Quilt Center Diagram, draw a straight line perpendicular to the A triangle base through the center of the points across the quilt center.

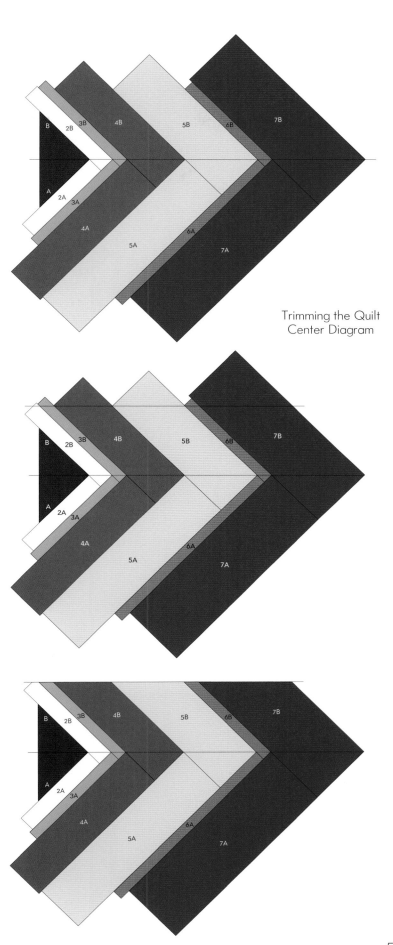

Trimming the Quilt Center Diagram

7. Measure 16-3/4" from the centerline up through the B section of the quilt center. Make several marks at this measurement along the B section. Join the marks into a straight line across the B section of the quilt center. Cut on the marked line to trim the excess fabric.

8. Measure 33-1/2" from the centerline down through the A section of the quilt center. Referring to step 6, mark the A section and trim the excess fabric.

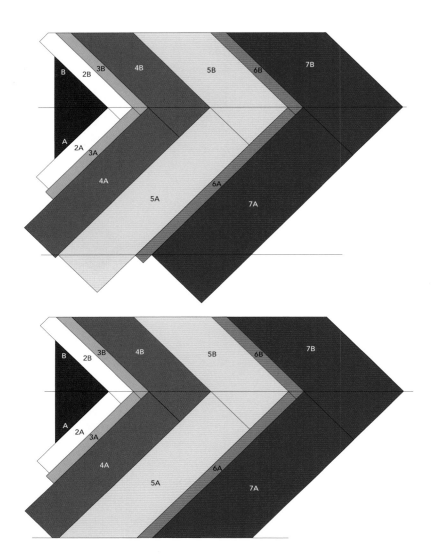

9. Square up the left side of the quilt center by drawing a line from the intersecting point of the 2B/3B seam at the top edge and the intersecting point of the 4A/5A seam at the bottom edge.

   **Note:** This line should be perpendicular to the center line.

   Cut on the marked line to trim the excess fabrics.

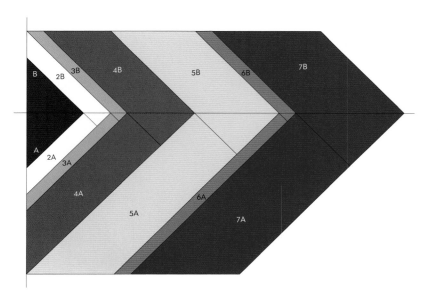

10. Beginning at the top edge of the angled 7B strip, measure 13" and mark. Beginning at the bottom edge of the angled 7A strip, measure 36-1/2" and mark. Draw a line from the 7B mark to the 7A mark. Cut on the drawn line to trim the excess fabric.

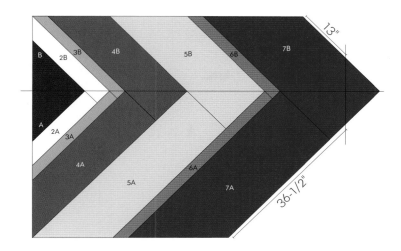

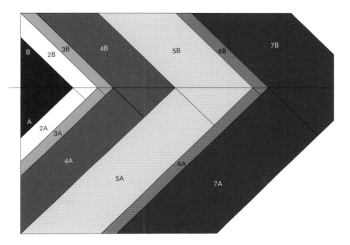

11. Aligning the raw edges, sew a green dot 8A strip to the geometric 7A rectangle. Press seams toward the strip. Sew the 9A-10A pieces to the A side of the quilt center in the same manner.

12. Referring to step 11, sew the 8B-9B pieces to the B side of the quilt center.

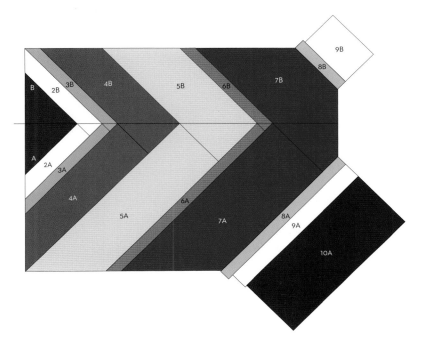

13. Square the upper and lower corners to complete the quilt center.

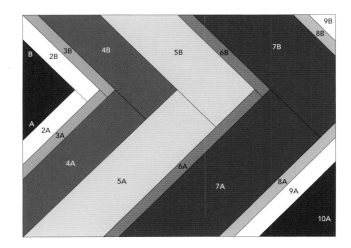

## Border and Quilt Assembly

**Note:** Measure the quilt center through the center to determine its width. **Cut all border strips to this length.**

1. Sew (2) charcoal dot 2" x WOF border strips together along one short end. Press the seam open. Make a total of 2 charcoal dot border strips.

2. Sew the white tonal 4-1/2" x WOF border strips together along one short end. Press the seam open.

3. Referring to step 2, make a 3" white tonal border strip, 16" gray/silver border strip, 11-1/2" gray/silver leaf border strip and 3-1/2" black tonal border strip.

4. Sew a charcoal dot strip, 4 1/2" white tonal strip, grey/silver leaf strip and black tonal strip together as shown to make the top border set.

5. Sew the 3" white tonal strip, a charcoal dot strip and gray/silver strip together as shown to make the bottom border set.

6. Sew the top border set to top (B side) of the quilt center. The charcoal dot strip is sewn to the top of the B side.

7. Sew the bottom border set to the bottom (A side) of the quilt center to complete the quilt top. The white tonal strip is sewn to the bottom of the A side.

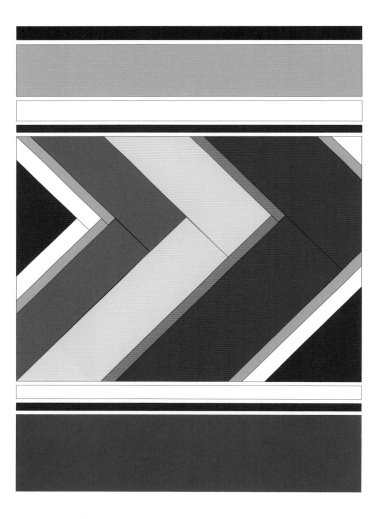

# Finishing

1. Sew the (2) 74" x WOF backing pieces together lengthwise. Press seam open. Layer quilt top, batting and backing together and baste. Tie, hand or machine quilt as desired.

2. Sew the (9) 2-1/4" x WOF binding strips together into one continuous strip. Press the strip in half lengthwise, wrong sides together, and sew to the raw edge of the quilt top. Fold over raw edges and hand stitch in place on back of quilt.

# City Center Steps Quilt

Designed and pieced by TailorMade by Design;
quilted by Sheri Zolar

Finished quilt size: 64-1/4" x 80"

Finished block size: 12-3/4"

## Yardage

1-1/8 yards dark multi-color print fabric

1/3 yard light blue tonal fabric

1/3 yard medium blue tonal #1 fabric

1/8 yard dark blue tonal fabric

7/8 yard turquoise tonal fabric

2-1/2 yards white print fabric

7/8 yard medium blue tonal #2 fabric

5 yards backing fabric

WOF = width of fabric
Read all instructions before beginning. Yardage is based on 44/45"-wide fabric. Cutting instructions include 1/4" seam allowance.

## Cutting

**Note:** As you cut, label each group of fabrics with its corresponding letter. This will help as you assemble the blocks.

From dark multi-color print fabric, cut:
(6) 4-3/4" x 13 1/4" A rectangles
(2) 13-1/4" x WOF border strips

From light blue tonal fabric, cut:
(6) 4-3/4" x 6-1/2" B1 rectangles

From medium blue tonal #1 fabric, cut:
(6) 4-3/4" x 6-1/2" B2 rectangles

From dark blue tonal fabric, cut:
(6) 2-1/4" D squares

From turquoise tonal fabric, cut:
(8) 3" x WOF strips.
    From 1 strip, cut: (4) 3" x 9" F strips
    From **each** of 2 strips, cut:
        (1) 3" x 9" F strip and (1) 3" x 26" J1 strip
    From **each** of 3 strips, cut:
        (1) 3" x 26" J1 strip and (1) 3" x 13-1/4" H1 strip
    From **each** of 2 strips, cut: (1) 3" x 38-3/4" K1 strip

From white print fabric, cut:
(6) 3" x 4-3/4" C rectangles
(6) 2-1/4" x 3" E rectangles
(6) 4-3/4" G squares
(7) 10-3/4" x WOF strips. From **each** of 2 strips, cut:
    (1) 10-3/4" x 26" J2 rectangle
    From **each** of 3 strips, cut:
    (1) 10-3/4" x 26" J2 rectangle and
    (1) 10-3/4" x 13-1/4" H2 rectangle
    From **each** of 2 strips, cut:
    (1) 10-3/4" x 38-3/4" K2 rectangle

From medium blue tonal #2 fabric, cut:
(4) 2" x WOF border strips
(8) 2-1/4" x WOF binding strips

From backing fabric, cut:
(2) 72" x WOF pieces

# Block Assembly

1. Sew a light blue B1 rectangle to a white G square to make a B1 set. Make a total of 6 B1 sets.

Make 6 B1 sets

2. Sew a white E rectangle to a dark blue D square to make an ED unit. Referring to the diagrams, sew a white C rectangle to the ED unit to make an EDC unit. Make a total of 6 EDC units.

Make 6 EDC unit

3. Referring to the diagram, sew a medium blue #1 B2 rectangle to an EDC unit to make a B2 set. Make a total of 6 B2 sets.

Make 6 B2 sets

4. Sew a B2 set to the left side of a B1 set to make a B set. Make a total of 6 B sets.

Make 6 B sets

5. Sew a turquoise F strip to the top of a B set to make an FB unit. Make a total of 6 FB units.

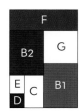

Make 6 FB units

6. Sew a dark multi-color A rectangle to the right side of an FB unit to make a Weave block. Make a total of 6 Weave blocks.

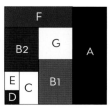

Make 6 Weave blocks

7. Sew a turquoise H1 strip to a white H2 rectangle to make an H block. Make a total of 3 H blocks.

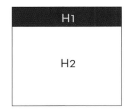

Make 3 H blocks

8. Sew a turquoise J1 strip to a white J2 rectangle to make a J block. Make a total of 5 J blocks.

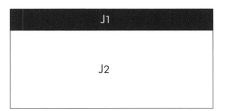

Make 5 J blocks

9. Sew turquoise K1 strip to a white K2 rectangle to make a K block. Make a total of 2 K blocks.

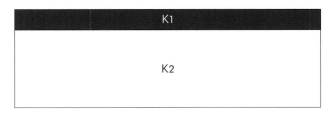

Make 2 K blocks

# Quilt Center Assembly

1. Lay out the blocks in rows as shown in the Quilt Center Assembly Diagram. Pay careful attention to the orientation of the blocks.

2. Sew the pieces together in rows. Press the seams in one direction.

3. Sew the rows together to complete the quilt center.

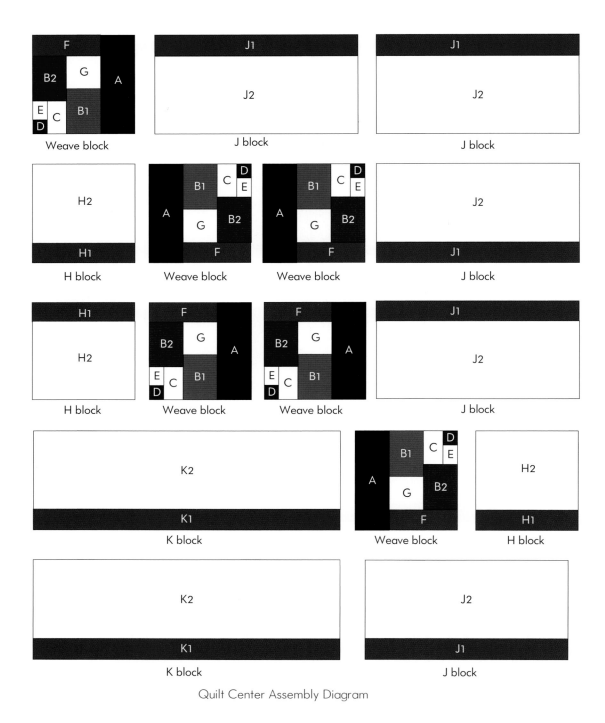

Quilt Center Assembly Diagram

## Border and Quilt Assembly

1. Sew the dark multi-color 13-1/4" x WOF border strips together along one short end. Press the seam open. Sew the strip to the bottom of the quilt center.

2. Sew (2) medium blue #2 border strips together along one short end. Press the seam open to make a top/bottom border strip. Make a total of 2 top/bottom border strips.

3. Sew the top/bottom border strips to the top and bottom of the quilt center. Trim all edges to complete the quilt top.

## Finishing

1. Sew the (2) 72" x WOF backing pieces together lengthwise. Press seam open. Layer quilt top, batting and backing together and baste. Tie, hand or machine quilt as desired.

2. Sew the (8) 2-1/4" x WOF binding strips together into one continuous strip. Press the strip in half lengthwise, wrong sides together, and sew to the raw edge of the quilt top. Fold over raw edges and hand stitch in place on back of quilt.

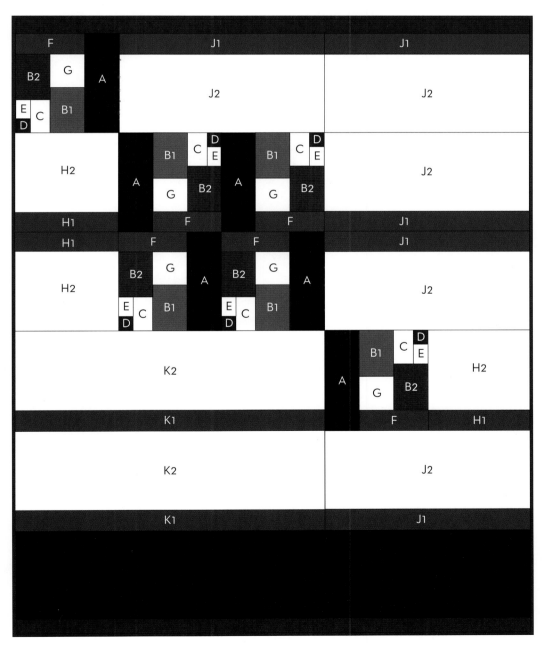

# Roundabout Quilt

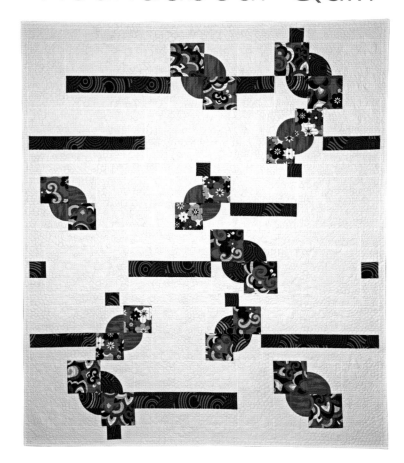

Designed and pieced by TailorMade by Design;
quilted by Sheri Zalar

Finished quilt size: 65" x 78"

Finished block size: 10" and 12"

## Yardage

3/4 yard large graphic print fabric

1/4 yard medium floral print fabric

1/4 yard black/silver spiral print fabric

1/4 yard red tonal fabric

5/8 yard red/black/silver spiral print fabric

4-3/4 yards white tonal fabric

4 yards backing fabric

1-1/2 yards 24"-wide fusible webbing

WOF = width of fabric
Read all instructions before beginning. Yardage is based on 44/45"-wide fabric. Cutting instructions include 1/4" seam allowance.

## Cutting

**Note:** As you cut, label each group of fabrics with its corresponding letter/number. This will help as you assemble the blocks and rows.

**From large graphic print fabric, cut:**
(10) 6-1/2" A squares
(4) 5-1/2" C squares

**From medium floral print fabric, cut:**
(6) 5-1/2" C squares

**From red/black/silver spiral print fabric, cut:**
(2) 3-1/2" x WOF strips.
   From 1 strip, cut: (2) 3-1/2" x 19-1/4" E strips
   From remaining strip, cut: (1) 3-1/2" x 15-1/2" I strip
      (1) 3-1/2" x 7-1/4" K strip
      (2) 3-1/2" H squares
(3) 3" x WOF strips.
   From 1 strip, cut: (2) 3" x 21-1/2" F strips
   From 1 strip, cut: (2) 3" x 12-1/2" G strips
      (1) 3" x 10-1/2" J strip
   From remaining strip, cut: (6) 3" L squares

**From white tonal fabric, cut:**
(2) 12-1/2" x WOF strips.
   From 1 strip, cut:
      (2) 12-1/2" x 15-1/2" W1 rectangles
   From remaining strip, cut:
      (5) 12-1/2" x 7-1/4" W2 strips
(2) 10-1/2" x WOF strips.
   From 1 strip, cut: (1) 10-1/2" x 22-1/2" W3 rectangle
      (2) 10-1/2" x 15" W4 rectangles

From remaining strip, cut: (1) 10-1/2" W5 square
      (1) 10-1/2" x 2-1/2" W6 strip
(4) 6-1/2" x WOF strips.
   From 1 strip, cut: (1) 6-1/2" x 19-1/4" E2 strip
      (1) 6-1/2" x 15-1/2" I2 strip
   From 1 strip, cut: (1) 6-1/2" x 19-1/4" E2 strip
      (1) 6-1/2" x 7-1/4" K2 strip
   From remaining 2 strips, cut:
      (10) 6-1/2" A squares
(4) 5-1/2" x WOF strips.
   From 1 strip, cut: (2) 5-1/2" x 21-1/2" F2 strips
   From 1 strip, cut: (2) 5-1/2" x 12-1/2" G2 strips
      (3) 5-1/2" C squares
   From 1 strip, cut: (7) 5-1/2" C squares
   From 1 strip, cut: (1) 5-1/2" x 10-1/2" J2 strip
(2) 3-1/2" x WOF strips.
   From 1 strip, cut: (2) 3-1/2" x 19-1/4" E strips
   From 1 strip, cut: (1) 3-1/2" x 15-1/2" I strip
      (1) 3-1/2" x 7-1/4" K strip
      (2) 3-1/2" x 6-1/2" H2 strip
      (2) 3-1/2" H squares
(9) 3" x WOF strips.
   From 1 strip, cut: (1) 3" x 31" W7 strip
      (1) 3" x 10-1/2" J strip
   From 1 strip, cut:
      (1) 3" x 25-1/2" W8 strip
      (1) 3" x 14-1/4" W9 strip
   From 1 strip, cut: (3) 3" x 14-1/4" W9 strips
   From 1 strip, cut: (1) 3" x 21-1/2" F strip
      (1) 3" x 12-1/2" G strip
   From 1 strip, cut: (1) 3" x 21-1/2" F strip
      (1) 3" x 12-1/2" G strip
   From 1 strip, cut: (1) 3" x 19-3/4" W10 strip
      (1) 3" x 14-1/4" W9 strip
   Sew the remaining 3" x WOF strips together end to end to make 1 strip. From the strip, cut:
      (2) 3" x 47-1/4" W11 strips
(7) 1-1/2" x WOF border strips
(8) 2-1/4" x WOF binding strips

**From backing fabric, cut:**
(2) 72" x WOF pieces

**Note:** Follow the manufacturer's instructions to apply fusible webbing to the wrong side of the black/silver spiral print and red tonal fabric before cutting.

**From black/silver spiral fabric, cut:**
(6) B using the templates on page 77
(2) D using the templates on page 77

**From red tonal fabric, cut:**
(4) B using the templates on page 77
(8) D using the templates on page 77

# Block Assembly

1. Remove the paper backing from a red tonal B and place it wrong side down on the right side of a white tonal A square. Match the corners' raw edges and press in place to make a red AB set. Make a total of 4 red AB sets.

Make 4 red AB sets

2. Referring to step 1, make a total of 6 black/silver AB sets, 8 red CD sets and 2 black/silver CD sets.

Make 6 black/silver AB sets     Make 8 red CD sets     Make 2 black/silver CD sets

3. Using a zigzag or decorative stitch and matching thread, appliqué the curved edge of the B and D pieces.

4. Sew a large graphic print A square to the left side of a red AB set as shown. Press the seam toward the A square to make unit A. Make a total of 4 unit A.

Make 4 unit A

5. Sew 2 unit A together as shown to make a red A block. Make a total of 2 red A blocks. Square the blocks to 12-1/2".

Make 2 red A blocks

6. Referring to steps 4-5 and the diagram, make 3 black A blocks.

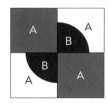

Make 3 black A blocks

7. Sew a medium floral C square to the left side of a red CD set as shown. Press the seam toward the C square to make unit C. Make a total of 6 unit C.

Make 6 unit C

8. Sew 2 unit C together as shown to make a floral C block. Make a total of 3 floral C blocks. Square the blocks to 10-1/2".

Make 3 floral C blocks

9. Using the large graphic print C square and referring to steps 7-8 and the diagram, make 1 black C block and 1 red C block.

Make 1 red C block     Make 1 black C block

10. Lay out a white tonal E strip, red/black/silver spiral E strip and white tonal E2 strip as shown. Sew the strips together. Press the seams toward the center strip to make an E block. Make a total of 2 E blocks.

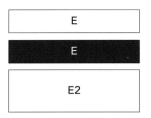

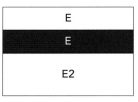

Make 2 E blocks

11. Referring to step 10 and the diagrams, make the following blocks using the white tonal and red/black/silver spiral strips with corresponding letters.

Make 2
F blocks

Make 2
G blocks

Make 2
H blocks

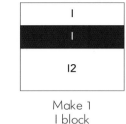

Make 1
I block

Make 1
J block

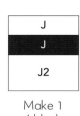

Make 1
K block

# Quilt Center Assembly

1. Referring to the Row Assembly Diagram on page 75, lay out the blocks, strips and rectangles in 10 rows as shown. Pay careful attention to the rotation of the blocks.

**Row 1:** W11 strip, L square, W9 strip

**Row 2:** W2 strip, red A block, W2 strip, E block, black A block, W2 strip

**Row 3:** F block, black C block, W5 square, floral C block, G block

**Row 4:** W8 strip, L square, W10 strip, L square, W9 strip

**Row 5:** H block, W1 rectangle, black A block, I block, W1 rectangle, H block

**Row 6:** W4 rectangle, G block, floral C block, W4 rectangle, red C block, W6 strip

**Row 7:** W9 strip, L square, W9 strip, L square, W7 strip

**Row 8:** J Block, floral C block, W3 rectangle, F block

**Row 9:** W2 strip, black A block, K block, red A block, E block, W2 strip

**Row 10:** W9 strip, L square, W11 strip


2. Sew the pieces together in row. Press the seams in each row in alternating directions.

3. Sew the rows together to complete the quilt center. Press the seams in one direction.

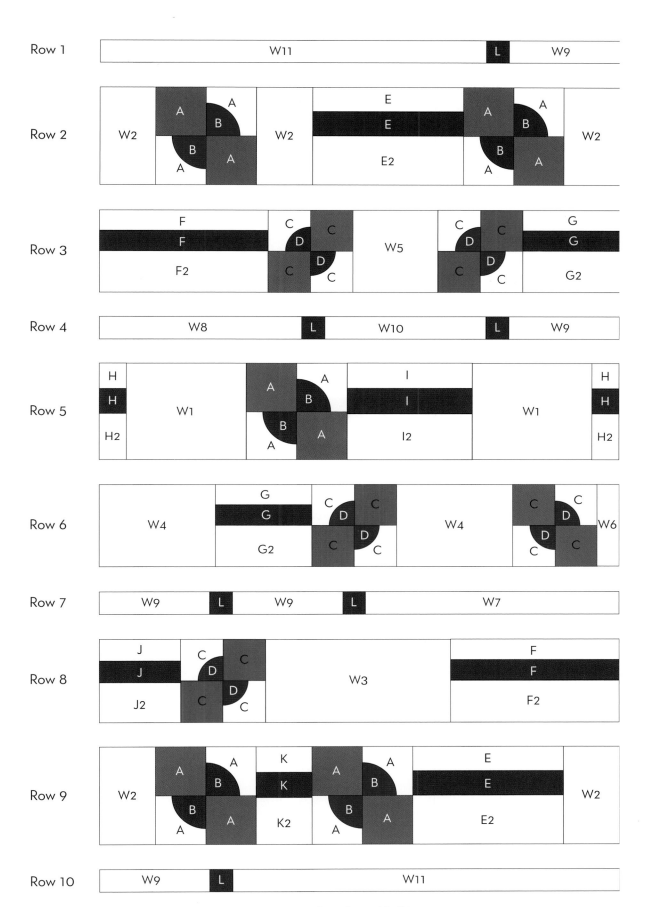

Row Assembly Diagram

## Border and Quilt Assembly

1. Sew (2) 1-1/2" x WOF white tonal border strips together along the short ends. Press the seam open to complete a side border. Make 2 side borders.

2. Sew the side borders to opposite sides of the quilt center. Trim the side borders even with the quilt top and bottom. Press the seams toward the borders.

3. Sew (2) 1-1/2" x WOF white tonal border strips together along the short ends. Press the seam open.

4. Sew the strip to the top of the quilt center. Trim even with the quilt sides and press seams toward the border.

5. Sew the trimmed strip to the remaining 1-1/2" x WOF white tonal border strip. Press the seam open. Sew the strip to the bottom of the quilt center. Trim even with quilt sides and press seams toward border to complete the quilt top.

## Finishing

1. Sew the (2) 72" x WOF backing pieces together lengthwise. Press seam open. Layer quilt top, batting and backing together and baste. Tie, hand or machine quilt as desired.

2. Sew the (8) 2-1/4" x WOF binding strips together into one continuous strip. Press the binding strip in half lengthwise, wrong sides together, and sew to the raw edge of the quilt top. Fold over raw edges and hand stitch in place on back of quilt.

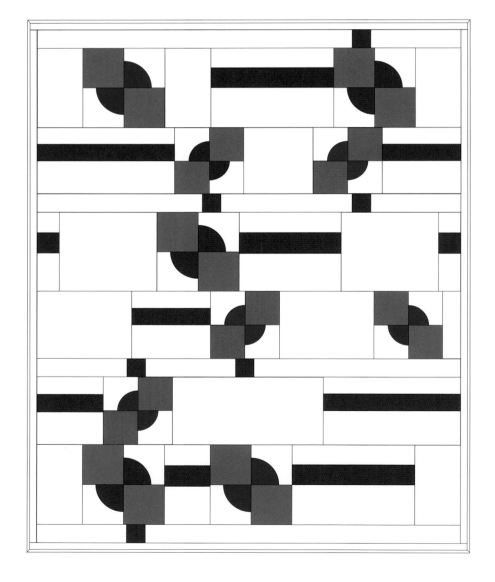

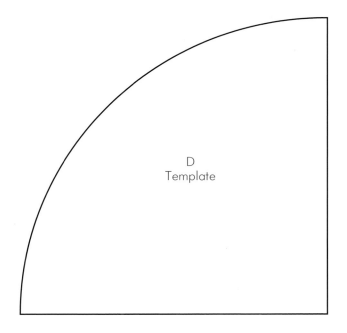

D
Template

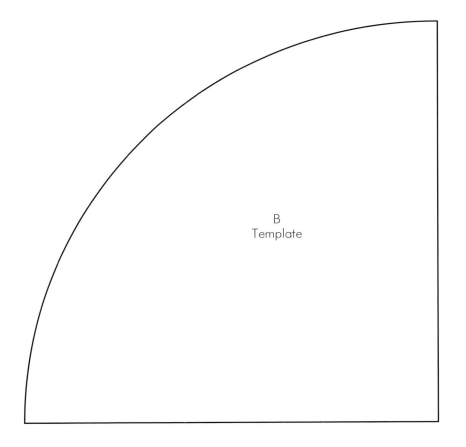

B
Template

# Colorations & Resources

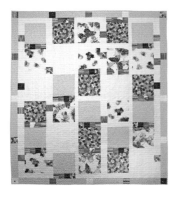

## Art in the Park Quilt 6

Original coloration:
Michael Miller Fabrics "Paintbox";
Kanvas Studio "Fleurish"

Optional coloration:
Contempo "Carina"

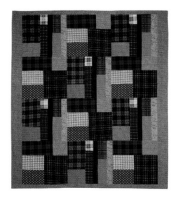

## October Nights Quilt 18

Original coloration:
Windham Fabrics "Flannel Elements"

Optional coloration: Benartex "On the Green"

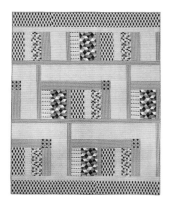

## City Blocks Quilt 24

Original coloration:
Windham Fabrics "Kinetics";
Benartex "Metallic Burlap"

Optional coloration:
Windham Fabrics "World Map"

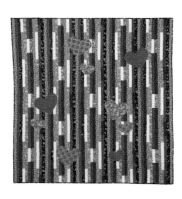

## Urban Retro Quilt 32

Original coloration:
Blend Fabrics "The Makers"

Optional coloration:
Windham Fabrics "WindSong"

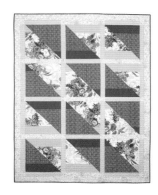

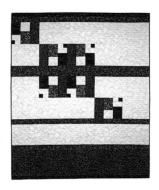
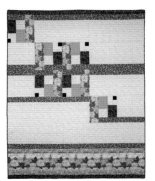
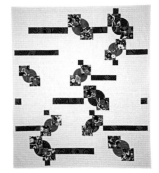
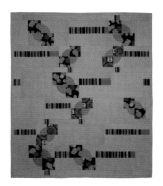

# Acknowledgements

We have always said it is the people in the quilting industry that make our job so much fun. We are truly blessed to have an incredible group of ladies who piece and quilt for us. We simply could not create what we do without their commitment and willingness to work within our creative chaos! Specifically, we would like to thank our long-arm quilters, Naomi Polzin, Sue Krause and Sheri Zalar, as well as the ladies that tested and pieced our second colorations, Sue Homan, Vicki Swanson, Jennifer Green, Julie Jergens and Theresa Vacek. A special thanks to Annie and Olivia who quietly fold, sort and organize so we don't drown in a sea of fabric. We would also like to thank Trina Severson of 507 Studio for her contribution of excellent urban living photos to complete our book.

# Resources

The manufacturers in the quilting fabric industry are truly the best! Thank you to all those that provided fabric for us to create these beautiful quilts – Benartex, Contempo, Kanvas Studio, Anna Griffin, Blend Fabrics, Michael Miller Fabrics, Windham Fabrics and Turtle Hand Batiks. Our creativity is sparked by each print you produce.

Visit the TailorMade by Design website at SewQuiltCraft.com

*Joanie*     *Melanie*

# About Us

Our mom, Marilyn Johnson loved to sew. We are so lucky she passed this love to us. It has given us the opportunity to work together and weave our creativity and sewing passion into careers we love.

Our company, TailorMade by Design, focuses on creating designs and projects to highlight our textile clients' newest fabric collections. We also work with clients to design and produce award winning Quilt Market booths. Recently we have started to offer our own patterns for sale and now have our second pattern book. We hope our pattern designs inspire and challenge each level of quilter.

Joanie and her husband Cody live south of Minneapolis in Farmington, Minnesota. Their son Zach is 21 and daughter Chloe is 19.

Melanie and her husband RJ live in the country just north of Peoria, Illinois. Their daughter Olivia is 23, son Eli is 21 and youngest son Emerson is 17.